Bygone LARKHALL

by

RICHARD STENLAKE

© Copyright 1992 Richard Stenlake
First published in the United Kingdom, 1992
By Richard Stenlake, 1 Overdale Street, Langside, Glasgow G42 9PZ
Tel: 041-632-2304

ISBN 1-872074-14-6

MONTGOMERY STREET, LARKHALL

LANARKSHIRE HERITAGE SERIES

INTRODUCTION

Little is known about the very early history of Larkhall. The lands which subsequently became the Parish of Dalserf, in which Larkhall is situated, were originally known as Meeheyn (Machan) and belonged to the ancient church of Cadihou (Cadzow). Later they belonged to the powerful Comyn family, who were forcefully dispossessed of them by Robert the Bruce. In 1314, King Robert gifted the lands of Cadzow and Machan to one Walter Fitzgilbert de Hamilton (sometimes referred to as Walter, son of Gilbert) in recognition of the support he had given Bruce during the Wars of Independence; Walter, whose family had held lands in Lanarkshire from 1294, had been employed by the English king as Governor of Bothwell Castle, but changed sides a little while after the Battle of Bannockburn! From him, the Dukes of Hamilton are descended.

The lands around Larkhall were in time dispersed to descendent branches of the Hamilton family (often referred to as 'cadet' branches). Whether related by blood or simply by marriage, all of these families bore or assumed the Hamilton name, thus promoting ties of kinship, a necessary method of self-preservation in violent and troubled times. Hence the proliferation of the Hamilton surname locally in the present day.

The Hamilton family's power and influence increased over the subsequent 250 years or so until the time of Mary Queen of Scots. The Hamiltons — it seems against their better judgement — loyally supported Mary who was thoroughly routed at the Battle of Langside (1568). Mary fled south through the lands of the Hamiltons. For being on the wrong side — the losing side basically — the local people suffered what local histories usually refer to as "great privations". Exactly what this means is unclear, although it is in this period that the Broomhill and Raploch estates fell into ruin, suggesting that the Hamiltons were stripped of their estates — or at least the lion's share of the estates' income — and the area was plunged into abject poverty.

The Hamiltons were subsequently troubled by a series of "wrong" decisions, few of which can have been of much benefit to the area and its people. The 1st Duke of Hamilton gained a duchy but lost his head on account of his support for Charles I. The 2nd Duke was killed in battle fighting the same cause two years later. The 4th Duke led the unsuccessful opposition to the 1707 Act of Union, prior to being despatched in a duel in 1712. The overall effect of all this upheaval was that the area failed to develop a more substantial economy until well into the 18th century.

Around this time, what we now know as Larkhall was little more than a handful of very small isolated settlements just as it had been when Pont had surveyed the area over a hundred years before. Pont's map, belatedly published in Blaeu's 1654 'Atlas of Scotland' shows recognisable names — 'Roploch' (Raploch), 'Milheach' (Millheugh), 'Skelliestoun', 'Struther', 'Althoofm' and, most importantly, 'Lakhouf' on a site at or near that of the Old Cross. This would seem to dispel the theory that Larkhall's original name was 'Laverockha' — the first appearance of the name in that form being on a 1773 map as 'Levrokhall'.

The Act of Union between England and Scotland, against which the 4th Duke had fought so hard, ironically sparked the ascendancy of the area once more. The Act enabled free trade between the two countries and some of the benefits of this rubbed off on the area. Larkhall still probably consisted of nothing more than a few wretched hovels. The main villages were at Millheugh and Dalserf where there would have been fishing and fruit-growing, although settlements principally grew at these locations because of their suitability as points to cross the rivers Avon and Clyde respectively. Despite growth in population, in 1755 the parish could hardly have been said to be crowded by its mere 765 people; today the population of Larkhall alone is over 16,000! After 1760, the increase was, however, quite dramatic. The agricultural revolution, with its novel methods of land enclosure and crop rotation, resulted in greater food production. More people could be fed by the land. By 1792, births in the parish were outstripping deaths by a ratio of 3:2 and the population had soared to 1100 souls.

With the population increasing, the land-owner at Dalserf from about 1774 followed a new policy of granting 99 year leases at Larkhall, but only one year leases at Dalserf. As a result, Dalserf village — originally a largish settlement running up the hillside above the present A72 road — fell into decay and the population gradually migrated to Larkhall.

By 1792, there were 100 weavers in the parish and 35 coal miners. Larkhall was given further impetus by the construction of the Ayr to Edinburgh Turnpike through the town in 1791. This happily coincided with a period of prosperity in the hand-loom weaving industry and caused a house building boom in which the village swelled to 100 houses.

After the Napoleonic Wars finished in 1815, post-war economic recession and inflation caused unemployment and political agitation in the town. The crisis reached its peak in the years 1819-20. Elsewhere, agitation turned into action and people took up arms — with tragic results. In Larkhall though, Telford's alterations and improvements to the Carlisle turnpike road brought much needed temporary employment and consequent financial relief to the inhabitants. This and the principles of thrift and co-operation engendered by the building society movement and the establishment of the victualling society helped the town through a difficult period as the fortunes of the handloom weaving industry gradually declined.

By 1840, Larkhall was a boom town once more. Building was taking place in several locations and the area was gripped by "the speculative spirit of the age" with the realisations that the parish was one large, accessible and easily wrought field of coal sited near to increasingly active ironworks and that a railway running from Glasgow to the north of England would almost certainly be built through the parish. It was. The town prospered, in time throwing up the usual assortment of public buildings, but strangely never achieving burgh status.

Coal-mining in the area reached its height during the Great War, but after the war the industry went into decline as pits became exhausted or unworkable. The government responded by including Lanarkshire as part of the Scottish Development Area and in 1939 the industrial estate was founded. Today, the mines are all shut, but Larkhall soldiers on with a mixture of light industry, commerce and dormitory accommodation for the workers of Glasgow, Hamilton and the neighbouring towns. Unemployment is high and the economy is once more in recession, but in Larkhall new houses are again being built and all eyes are on nearby Mossend where the new Euro-Rail Terminal will be built and nearby Motherwell in or near which an Enterprise Zone may appear. The river Avon is to get a clean and even the railway is maybe coming back! A combination of affordable housing, good communications and new industry may regenerate Larkhall once more just like it did in the 1790s and the 1840s.

Richard Stenlake. January 1992

The old village of Larkhall dates from about 1774 when the first feus were given off in what are now Hamilton Street, Duke Street, Drygate Street, and Wellgate Street. The oldest properties appear to be in Hamilton Street, but it is hard to tell. This view dates from about 1905, maybe a year or two earlier, and looks north up Drygate Street towards the Old Cross. Hamilton Street and the Drygate formed part of the 1791 Ayr-Edinburgh turnpike road and this was also the route from Glasgow to Carlisle. Nowadays, the Old Cross features a mini-roundabout and it seems hard to believe that at one time the Drygate was an international trade route! Today, the cottage on the left at the north side of Montgomery Street survives and has been extended, but the two-storey building on the right has gone. A petrol station is sited to the right of the two tots.

4

Larkhall Cross & Wellgate St.

Today's traveller going from Ayr to Edinburgh would be unlikely to end up in the town, but in 1791 the turnpike road between these two places followed a route taking in Kilmarnock, Eaglesham, East Kilbride, Hamilton and Larkhall as it headed towards its crossing point on the Clyde upstream. By a happy accident of location, Larkhall was simply in the way on a route designed to take in existing centres of population. The Ayr-Edinburgh route was revised in 1819 when a new turnpike running via Cumnock, Muirkirk, Strathaven, Stonehouse and Shawsburn was constructed. Larkhall's first bypass! Any detrimental effect to the town was offset by Telford's new north-south turnpike which was re-routed along London Street, Union Street and on southwards. This created a 'new' centre of the town and the New Cross, as time wore on and it became more important, simply came to be known as 'The Cross'.

BRANDON SERIES

CROSS LARKHALL.

A carelessly captioned postcard (Cross Larkhall and not an angry person in sight!) of Union Street looking towards The Cross circa 1903. The tide of progress had hit this part of the town some twenty years previously when most of the original weavers' cottages made way for these two-storey buildings. The two cottages visible here have survived into the present day, the one on the right now a hi-fi shop. The wall on the left, here seen stubbornly resisting the building trend of the day, has now gone and the gap site is fronted by billboards. Still in place, at the junction with Raploch Street, are the easily-missed but interesting finger-post signs erected by the County Council around the turn of the century.

6

Looking the same way from outside Burns the stationers, which at this time (circa 1904) appears to have also housed the Post Office. Larkhall Post Office opened around 1838. In 1893, William Burns was postmaster and it was located in Raploch Street before moving round the corner onto Union Street. Today the P.O. is housed on the other side of the road in a modern and no doubt functional red-brick building which must be to somebody's taste.

Raploch Street in 1899. In olden times, a tree-lined avenue led to Raploch Castle following a route by the present-day Wellgate, Raploch Street and Raploch Road. The castle fell into ruins in the early 18th century. Its dovecot reportedly lasted until around 1900. Also despatched around this time was the 'Raploch Bush' — not a bush at all, but an ancient yew tree with no fewer than nine stems that had offered choice for the hangman in the performance of his grim duties.

Union Street from The Cross circa 1904, looking not unlike it does today. Thirty years before, the view would have been strikingly different with rows of 'weavers' cottages' lining both sides of the street. Looking very out of place here beside its late Victorian 'neighbours' is a thatched cottage at the corner of Montgomery Street.

At Martinmas, 1824, the "Larkhall Building Society" was formed with 29 members. As funds became available, the society built on both sides of what is now London Street. About half of these cottages remain. The rest were swept away by redevelopment in the 1890s. Some of their replacements have, in turn, not lasted a century resulting in a disjointed look to parts of London Street.

Union Street, Larkhall.

In the summer of 1905, transport to and from Larkhall was made doubly easier in the space of a few weeks. On 30th June, the Caledonian Railway ran its first services into the new Central Station and on 23rd July the Lanarkshire Tramways reached the town. The tramway linked into Glasgow's system at Cambuslang enabling the determined passenger to travel as far afield as Paisley or Yoker by tram.

Competition from buses squeezed tramway systems everywhere in Britain in the 1920s. Buses were faster and could offer a wider choice of routes and destinations. The inevitable happened — the last tram ran in Larkhall in September 1928 and in 1932 the Lanarkshire Tramway Company was absorbed by S.M.T.

UNION STREET, LARKHALL

More 'weavers' cottages'. These ones dated from around the 1840s. They were not, of course, all inhabited by weavers. The term 'weaver's cottage' describes the style and not the use of the building, although many such cottages did indeed belong to weavers. The row on the left has been replaced by some dull two-storey brick buildings, while that on the right has made way for a characterless single level row of modern shop units.

13

Looking the other way. On the right, it looks much the same today, but on the left ... oh dear ... everything between the camera and the church has gone.

Union Street from Charing Cross circa 1912. Before the railways came — and changed everything — Larkhall was on a number of stagecoach routes. The London Mail passed through the town as did a daily stagecoach between Glasgow and Lanark. Charing Cross probably owes its name to these coaching origins. The village of Halfway (now absorbed into Cambuslang) was I am told so-called because it was halfway between Charing Cross, Glasgow and Charing Cross, Larkhall.

The Empire Theatre opened in 1910 as a variety theatre and cinema. The 1920s was a boom period for picture houses. The Empire prospered as did its rival — The Grand Central on Union Street. The Empire devoted less and less time to variety acts and concentrated increasingly on showing movies. The arrival of the talkies necessitated the installation of a sound system in the Empire in 1930. During that same year, the competing Grand Central was ravaged by fire.

UNION STREET, LARKHALL.

The Grand Central was subsequently rebuilt. It later became The Regal as pictured here in the 1950s. Both The Empire and The Regal showed films into the 1960s, but, rather like the competing tram and railway before them, the competing businesses were overtaken by a third party technological upstart — television. The Empire survives as The Regal Bingo Hall. Its rival was not so lucky and in its place today are Stepek's, the TSB, and the entrance to the Gateway supermarket.

Police Station

Published by A. Brown, Larkhall

Larkhall

Arguably the most interesting building in Larkhall, the Police Station dates from 1901. It is a bizarre architectural hotch-potch with its recessed bay windows, Charles Rennie MacKintosh style lettering, baronial features and art nouveau railings. It may be the work of architects McWhannell and Rogerson who were responsible for the similar Royal Samaritan Hospital in Glasgow's Victoria Road.

POLICE STATION, LARKHALL.

Next to the Police Station is the old Fire Station. It dates from 1911 when Lanark County Council added four brigades to "our county equipment" operating out of four main stations at Shettleston, Bellshill, Larkhall and Lanark. The Larkhall brigade was responsible for the town plus Glassford, Stonehouse, Avondale, Dalziel, Cambusnethan and Carluke! "All important populous places can be reached within 15 minutes, and outlying districts in less than half an hour"

Each station was equipped with a petrol motor fire engine and pump. The 75 brake horse power fire engines could reach a dizzy 35 miles per hour! They were crewed principally by off-duty policemen, augmented by local tradesmen. The Fire Brigade commenced work on 1st February 1911.

NEW CENTRAL STATION, LARKHALL.

Larkhall's relationship with the railway has truly been stop-start. In the 1840s, the Caledonian Railway first brought a Bill before Parliament, but it was defeated. A second attempt, in 1847, was successful, but at this time many railways had been recently built, exhausting available capital and the scheme had to be abandoned because of lack of funds. When a line was built, it ran via Larkhall East Station. The Hamilton to Strathaven line was routed via Quarter and Larkhall town itself appeared to have been effectively by-passed. In 1897, however, the Caledonian Railway decided to run a second line to Strathaven via Larkhall and Stonehouse. The benefit of hindsight can throw no light on the reasons for what seemed to be an incredibly extravagant and almost pointless exercise. Among other costs, the project involved the building of two vastly expensive viaducts — only to take in two extra settlements before reaching a town the railway already served by another perfectly adequate route. The first trains on this folly arrived at Larkhall on Larkie Fair Day 1905.

Larkhall Central Station

In November 1963, the grim reaper of railways, Dr. Beeching, announced his closure plans for the Larkhall lines. There were howls of protest from all sides and there was a stay of execution, but it was just buying time. Bus operators, the main beneficiaries of closure, helpfully offered 'train bus' services. By now, despite whatever local protest there might be, the coffin lid was being hammered down firmly. Larkhall East was renamed Larkhall Goods, but in 1964 was then closed to all goods except minerals (principally coal). The last train from Larkhall Central ran on 2nd October 1965 and the station buildings were demolished in 1968. Today, the station is a graveyard for 'dead' supermarket trolleys and a haunt for under-age drinkers and goodness knows what else. Incredibly though, the railway is maybe coming back, at least to Larkhall. The cost is estimated at £4m and the debate continues.

New Academy, Larkhall.

The story of education in Larkhall is one of a growing population continually outstripping the resources provided. In 1792, when the schoolmaster had to cope with his 40 to 60 pupils, there was yet no schoolhouse in the parish.

Once the Academy was founded, its roll grew and grew and it was soon bursting at the seams. A second storey had to be added in 1884, but still the numbers swelled and a new building opened in 1896. This in turn had to be extended only six years later. Today, the Academy appears to have come to rest at its latest site at Gallowhill. The 'New' Academy pictured here lies empty and shuttered.

22

Glory days — Larkhall Academy Football Team in 1907, winners that year of the Hamilton and District Cup behind which they pose.

J McColl   Marshall   Gibb   Anderson   Hamilton   Frame   CW Thomson

        Tait   Stewart   Wilson

        Lochhead   D Stewart   Watson

"HANDLOOM WEAVING."

When a twister, a-twisting, will twist him a twist,   But if one of the twines of the twist doth untwist,
For the twisting his twist he three twines doth intwist;   The twine that untwisteth, untwisteth the twist.

By the 1790s, handloom weaving had grown to be far and away the main occupation in the area, especially so in Larkhall. One in eleven of the parish population was a weaver. With high rates for piece-working being paid by manufacturers desperate to get the finished cloth onto the market, weaving had become a prosperous occupation. It had the added attraction of being an easy one to enter; no apprenticeship was necessary and it only took a little effort to learn how to weave plain fabrics. This combination of easy entry and financial reward resulted in a flood of new entrants to the trade. Inevitably, some were prepared to accept lower piece-rates and consequently this caused a gradual erosion in the weaver's standard of living. It reached crisis point in 1812. A bitter national strike which lasted into 1813 was only finally broken by the imprisonment of the strike leaders. From then on, the lot of a handloom weaver was not a happy one, the prosperity of yore turning over the years into an increasingly desperate poverty. The introduction of power looms and factory weaving in the 1840s finished the handloom weaving industry off, although there was the odd diehard (like the one pictured here — actually from the Strathaven area) who carried on into the era of photography.

SHAWSBURN & PUBLIC SCHOOL FROM ENAMEL WORKS.

At Shawsburn, miners' rows stood next to fields. Nearby, to transport the coal, was Dalserf Station, originally called 'Ayr Road'. The Enamel Works, referred to in the postcard's title, manufactured glazed draining tiles. It operated from the mid 19th century until the late 1920s.

LANARKSHIRE INDUSTRY

MINERS ON CAGE READY TO DESCEND   SCENE AT LANARKSHIRE MINE Nº1

There was coal-mining in the area by the 1790s, although these would have been one man or one family operations. The earliest pits were located at Nityard, Drygate, Raploch, Old Buffy and Skellyburn. By 1840, these little operations had been superceded by larger-scale concerns and there were 8 or 9 collieries in the parish, with plans afoot for many more. Even before the arrival of the railways, coal was being 'exported' as far afield as Lanark and Cambuslang. In the decades that followed, the full exploitation of the coalfield began and coal-mining became the principal occupation reaching a height of activity during World War One. The industry then went into decline. Pictured here is a group of miners at a Lanarkshire pithead circa 1903.

LANARKSHIRE INDUSTRY

PONY HAULING HUTCHES

SCENE IN A LANARKSHIRE MINE NO 3

Perhaps the most famous personality associated with the Larkhall miners was Robert Smillie. Smillie spent fifteen years working in the Larkhall pits, in his later years becoming an activist. He became agent for the Larkhall miners and President of the Lanarkshire Miners' County Organisation. He went on to become President of the Scottish Miners' Federation and Chairman of The Scottish Union Trades Congress among other positions. He and the better-known Keir Hardie were instrumental in forming the Independent Labour Party and the memory of both men lives on in Larkhall street names.

Muir Street, Larkhall

Muir Street looking east circa 1912. This view looks down towards what was once the separate village of Pleasance. These days, building societies appear almost indistinguishable from banks. One leading society was recently honest enough to give up all pretences and turned itself into a bank! But it was not always so. Larkhall was famous for its building societies. In 1921, there were 3,300 houses in Larkhall, most of which were owner-occupied. Little wonder that Larkhall men were called "Wee Lairds o' Larkie". It was at High Pleasance that the first house was completed in 1816 by the two-year old Larkhall and Pleasance Building Society. The society was formed because of the huge upsurge in demand for houses and weavers' shops caused by the return of demobilised soldiers from the Napoleonic Wars.

28

MUIR STREET, LARKHALL.

Muir Street looking west towards Gorbals Cross circa 1918. High Pleasance and Low Pleasance were better known at one time as the High and Low Gorbals. The name is said to derive from when the building society houses were being built and progress was inspected by a gentleman from the Gorbals in Glasgow. His arrival was heralded by the shout "Here's the Gorbals coming". So the story goes anyway.

The building societies operated in a simple and mutual manner. By 1840, the members of the Larkhall and Pleasance Society had all been installed in their houses, owned them as their private property and the society had consequently been dissolved — a far cry from today when "your home is at risk if you do not keep up repayments" on the loans their junk-mail tries to tempt you to take.

Church Street, Larkhall.

By 1840, no fewer than three building societies were busy constructing houses in Larkhall. There were further building booms in the late 1850s (fuelled by the arrival of the railways) and in the early 1870s when coal pits were further developed occasioning the time of "the big wages". The total effect of all this building was to connect up all the little hamlets, rows of houses and dwellings in the locale to form what has been called "the biggest village in Scotland".

The Machan Road in 1899. Note the thatched roofs on two of the cottages. Such roofs could be seen in parts of Lanarkshire into the present century, although they were by that time obsolete and rapidly disappearing — by 1904, the ones shown here had been replaced with roof tiles.

In the 1820s, there was a brewery at Machan, but it was not a success and the buildings used by the failed venture became weavers' shops.

Machan Pond about 1904. This pleasure pond was located alongside the Machan Road and the site is now underneath part of the Strutherhill housing scheme.

Westerton Avenue looking towards Machan Road. Strutherhill dates from the inter-war years and was built under the National Rehousing Scheme, often known as the 'Houses fit for Heroes' programme. This view looks much the same today except that, as books like this always point out, the railings went during the war in the scrap iron drive. This was a morale-raising device for the home front, to make everybody feel involved in the war effort. The railings were never made into the promised tanks etc. and if only somebody had bothered to label them all, they could have been returned after the war.

Hareleeshill in 1906.

Mason Street, Hareleeshill, in the 1930s.

The houses in Burnhead date from the last phase of building society construction towards the end of the 19th century. The view is not that much changed today, although some of the houses have had dormers added. While no doubt these provide much-needed extra room, they do little for the look of the street.

PUBLIC PARK & WAR MEMORIAL, LARKHALL.

203335.J

The War Memorial sits in 2½ acres of ground, which were gifted by the Duke of Hamilton. The monumental sculptors, Scott and Rae, were responsible for its design and its construction from Creetown granite. It was unveiled in November 1921.

MacNeil Street dates from 1870, is seen here around 1912 and it all looks much the same today!

As one descends the Millheugh Brae, on the left is Braehead Avenue, another street of 19th century building society houses. It was at Braehead that the Rev. John McMillan, after whom the Covenanters are often known as McMillanites, resided for a while. Braehead House was used as a meeting-house by upwards of 30 people, but later fell into ruin and was demolished. McMillan is buried in the parish churchyard at Dalserf.

A tranquil Millheugh Brae in 1899. The origins of Millheugh are sketchy and obscure, but the village is thought to date from the early 17th century. The derivation of the name is simple — heuch or heugh (steep glen with overhanging sides) where mill is located.

Millheugh, showing River Avon. *Larkhall.*

As well as the mill (or mills), the other early industries at Millheugh were fruit-growing and fishing. Salmon were at one time plentiful in the River Avon, but by 1840 the New Statistical Account was moved to observe "very few are now caught in any of the waters above Glasgow". A combination of new dams, night-spearing and river pollution by lime and chemicals from dyeworks was blamed.

Millheugh, Larkhall

A printwork was founded at Avonbank in 1796, but was fairly short-lived. There was a dispute over pollution of the river, presumably by owners downstream, and the proprietor went away to Busby. Several other luckless ventures ensued, including a distillery started by John Burns of Machan (he of failed brewery fame). Around 1840, the dam was heightened and this elaborate system of lades and run-offs was constructed to power the undershot wheel in the new bleachworks which were about to open.

Millheugh, from the Stepping Stones.

30735. J.V.

1899 and it seems that just about the whole village has turned out to pose for Valentine's photographer. Generations of Millheugh children must have been talked into digging the garden by the true story of the earthenware pot dug up in the village in 1830. The pot contained brass, copper and silver coins from the reigns of Elizabeth, James I and Charles I, perhaps either plundered loot or hidden to avoid such a fate befalling it.

Glengowan & Avon Bank Bleach Works, Larkhall.

The bleach works in their heyday, pictured about 1906. Around this time, several hundred people, mainly women, worked here. The works closed in the 1920s and a new private housing estate now occupies the site.

On the Avon, Larkhall

There can be little dispute that Millheugh is the most attractive and charming corner of Larkhall and the river acts as a magnet, drawing local people to pass the time of day there. So it seems it has always been.

The old Millheugh Bridge, built in 1790 to replace a ferry, was said to be, at 80 feet, the largest single spanned bridge in Scotland. Its deteriorating condition had already caused sufficient alarm to warrant some renovation in 1933, but in November 1934 it collapsed into the river. Two men had "narrow escapes". Apparently, one had just crossed the bridge while the other was just approaching. No doubt the story lost nothing in the telling either!

The Clove Mill was situated on the north side of the Powforth Burn near to its confluence with the River Avon at Millheugh. Its function is revealed by the other name, by which it was known — The Spice Mill. Its heyday is thought to have been in the 1850s and 1860s. This picture dates from around 1912 by which time the mill was out of use. Now only traces of the mill and its bridge remain.

The Broomhill Estate and its history of tragedy and misfortune dates from 1473, when John Hamilton became proprietor of Broomhill and Machane Muir. 1568 found his descendant, Sir John Hamilton fighting on the side of Queen Mary at Langside. As a result, his castle (actually called The Castle of Auld Machan) was burnt to the ground. The Broomhill estate subsequently fell into decay.

In the 17th century, the Birnies were in possession and then in the 1820s the estate was sold to James Bruce, a local man returning home with the pile he had made in India. But the most notorious Broomhill tale concerns the Black Lady, the mistress of Captain MacNeil, who disappeared suddenly and whose ghostly form still haunts Broomhill and Millheugh. New evidence suggests that the story may well have its basis in truth. Broomhill House was demolished early this century, but the story refuses to die.

The Public Park at Braehead in 1937.

Viaduct over the "Avon", Larkhall, (The Highest Bridge in Scotland.)

44592.JV.

Towering over Morgan Glen is the awesome Larkhall or Broomhill Viaduct, built in 1904 by Arrol Bros. of Glasgow. The bridge has six spans, the longest of which is 170 feet. The total length of the bridge is 530 feet. It has six piers, erected on bases of concrete 52 feet long, 32 feet broad and sunk 25 and 60 feet below the ground.

At 170 feet from rail level to the stream below, the viaduct was reckoned to be the highest bridge in Scotland and the second highest in Britain. These very features now make it a favoured haunt of abseilers.

ASHGILL.

On an 1816 map, 'Gillhead' is marked, but the mining village of Ashgill dates from the late 19th century. The Post Office (the building behind the trees with the barely discernible people outside) opened in July 1899. Unlike today's mechanised and vague 'Clyde Valley' postmarks, little Ashgill had its own (now scarce) postmark with which all outgoing mail was hand-stamped.

This was Duncan's shop in Red Row, Ashgill. It is long demolished and was located where the new estate is on the left-hand side of the road to Netherburn.

Coal-mining on the Duke of Hamilton's Netherburn Farm commenced in the late 1830s. The Duke constructed a new road to connect the colliery with the Lanark Road. In 1856, the Caledonian Railway opened its Motherwell-Lesmahagow branch line, which took in several mining settlements including Netherburn. It can have come as little surprise when the line closed to passenger traffic in September 1951 — in 1950 the number of passengers carried daily to Larkhall was a mere 14. The original Netherburn Post Office, seen here, first opened for business on 25th February 1880.

Honey Comb Bridge Netherburn.

Today, the Post Office is situated in the "new" Netherburn, the post-war scheme built to house incoming Rolls-Royce workers. Its Honeycomb Place is named after this distinctively shaped little bridge. The bridge crossed the Honeycomb Burn which runs to the west of Netherburn and was replaced only a few years ago.

Hareleeshill Road looking east from what is now its junction with Field Road circa 1908. Today, the field has drowned in a sea of local authority four in a block houses and in the foreground the daisies have gone to make room for a pizza takeaway.

SOME FURTHER READING

Cormack, Ian L. Lanarkshire Tramways, 1971
McLellan, Jack Larkhall Its Historical Development, 1979
Larkhall Victuallying Society Ltd Centenary Souvenir, 1921

Old Statistical Account, 1792
New Statistical Account, 1845
Third Statistical Account, 1960

I owe thanks to the staffs of Larkhall and Hamilton libraries for their assistance, also to James Ross of Lesmahagow for his help. The illustrations on pages 25 and 53 are from his collection.